50 Delicious Quick Bread Recipes

(50 Delicious Quick Bread Recipes - Volume 1)

Lula Chambers

Copyright: Published in the United States by Lula Chambers/ © LULA CHAMBERS

Published on December, 02 2020

All rights reserved. No part of this publication may be reproduced, stored in retrieval system, copied in any form or by any means, electronic, mechanical, photocopying, recording or otherwise transmitted without written permission from the publisher. Please do not participate in or encourage piracy of this material in any way. You must not circulate this book in any format. LULA CHAMBERS does not control or direct users' actions and is not responsible for the information or content shared, harm and/or actions of the book readers.

In accordance with the U.S. Copyright Act of 1976, the scanning, uploading and electronic sharing of any part of this book without the permission of the publisher constitute unlawful piracy and theft of the author's intellectual property. If you would like to use material from the book (other than just simply for reviewing the book), prior permission must be obtained by contacting the author at author@rosemaryrecipes.com

Thank you for your support of the author's rights.

Content

50 AWESOME QUICK BREAD RECIPES .. 4

1. 15 Minute Scones Recipe 4
2. Bacon Cinnamon Rolls Recipe 4
3. Bisquick Banana Bread Recipe..................... 4
4. Blueberry Scones Recipe 5
5. Buttery Cinnamon Brown Sugar Rolls Recipe 5
6. Cheddar And Onion Scones Recipe 6
7. Cheese Fondue With Crusty Rolls Recipe .. 6
8. Chocolate Chip Scones Recipe 6
9. Cinnamon Apple Raisin Bread Recipe 7
10. Cinnamon Jam Donut Muffins Recipe 7
11. Cinnamon Raisin Scones Recipe 7
12. Cinnamon Roll Bites Recipe 8
13. Cinnamony Carrot Pumpkin Sweet Potato Bread Recipe.. 8
14. Coconut Almond Bread Pudding Recipe ... 9
15. De Lish Bagel Bites Recipe 9
16. Donut Muffins Recipe.................................... 10
17. Easy Caramel Sticky Buns Recipe 10
18. Easy Donuts Recipe.. 11
19. Easy Lemonade Scones Recipe.................... 11
20. Easy Raisin Bran Quick Bread Recipe....... 11
21. Fluffy Easy Donuts Surprise Recipe........... 12
22. French Toast Recipe....................................... 12
23. Isaiahs Toaster Grilled Cheese Recipe 12
24. Lazy Maple Sticky Buns Recipe 13
25. Lemon Verbena Scones Recipe 13
26. MUFFINS THAT TASTE LIKE DONUTS Recipe 13
27. Maple Oatmeal Scones Recipe..................... 14
28. Mini Crescent Cinnamon Rolls Recipe 14
29. Oatmeal Raisin Quick Bread Recipe.......... 15
30. Oatmeal Scones Recipe................................. 15
31. One Bowl Banana Bread Recipe 16
32. Orange Praline Quick Bread Recipe.......... 16
33. Peachy Cinnamon Rolls Recipe 17
34. Port Elizabeth Scones Recipe 17
35. Pumpkin Beer Quick Bread Recipe From Lv Anderson Recipe 18
36. Pumpkin Walnut Breakfast Bread Recipe.18
37. Quick Donuts Recipe 18
38. Quick Raisin Bread Pudding Recipe.......... 19
39. Quick And Easy Donuts Recipe.................. 19
40. Quick And Easy Scones Recipe................... 19
41. Raisin Bread Recipe....................................... 20
42. Snickerdoodle Banana Bread Recipe......... 20
43. Sorta Quick Cinnamon Rolls Recipe 21
44. Strawberry Scones Recipe 22
45. Super Simple Scones Recipe 22
46. Vegan Bran Raisin Bread Recipe 23
47. Walnut And Cheddar Scones Recipe 23
48. Bagel Sandwich Recipe 24
49. Lemonade Scones Recipe............................. 24
50. Ooey Gooey Breakfast Bagel Recipe 24

INDEX 26
CONCLUSION 28

50 Awesome Quick Bread Recipes

***

1. 15 Minute Scones Recipe

Serving: 6 | Prep: | Cook: 10mins | Ready in:

Ingredients

- 1 1/4 c. flour
- 1 1/4 tsp. baking powder
- 1/2 tsp. salt
- 2 tsp. sugar
- 2 tblsp. margarine or butter
- 1 egg
- 1/4 c. milk
- 1/4 c. raisins, craisins, chopped dried apricots, or chocolate chips (optional)
- sugar or cinnamon sugar

Direction

- Preheat oven to 450 degrees.
- Grease an 8 in. round cake pan.
- Mix the dry ingredients.
- Cut in the margarine.
- Beat the egg and milk and mix into the dry ingredients till dough holds.
- Add the fruit or chips if desired.
- Form into ball and knead 12 times.
- Place in pie pan and pat into 6 in. circle, 3/4 inch deep.
- Cut into 4 to 6 wedges, NOT all the way through.
- Sprinkle top with sugar or mixture of cinnamon/sugar.
- Bake 8-10 minutes or till golden.
- Serve warm with extra butter, jam and tea or coffee.

2. Bacon Cinnamon Rolls Recipe

Serving: 6 | Prep: | Cook: 22mins | Ready in:

Ingredients

- 1 sheet puff pastry, thawed for 40 minutes at room temp
- flour for rolling out puff pastry
- 1/2 stick butter, softened
- 1/2 cup brown sugar
- 1/4 cup white sugar
- 2 tablespoons cinnamon, ground
- 6 slices bacon, cooked crisply and chopped

Direction

- Preheat oven to 400 degrees.
- Roll the thawed puff pastry sheet on a floured surface to 1/8 inch thick.
- Mix the sugars and cinnamon in a small bowl.
- Spread the softened butter onto the rolled out pastry.
- Sprinkle with the sugar mixture.
- Cover with the chopped, crisp bacon.
- Roll the dough up and into a log and slice into 6 equal portions.
- Spray a 6 cup muffin pan with cooking spray and place a roll into each cup.
- Sprinkle with a bit more of the sugar mixture.
- Bake 20 -25 minutes in 400 degree oven.

3. Bisquick Banana Bread Recipe

Serving: 0 | Prep: | Cook: 60mins | Ready in:

Ingredients

- 1/3 cup vegetable oil
- 1-1/2 cups mashed ripe banana (about 3 large)

- 1/2 tsp vanilla
- 3 eggs
- 2-1/3 cups Bisquick baking mix
- 1 cup sugar
- 1/2 cup chopped nuts (optional)

Direction

- HEAT oven to 350 degrees
- GREASE bottom of loaf pan, 9x5x3, generously
- BEAT all ingredients vigorously with spoon 30 sec. Pour batter into pan.
- BAKE until wooden pick inserted in center comes out clean, 55 to 65 min.
- COOL 5 min, loosen sides of loaf from pan, remove from pan.
- High altitude: Heat oven to 375, decrease baking mix to 2 cups and sugar to 2/3 cup. Add 1/4 cup Gold Medal all-purpose flour. Bake 50-55 min.

4. Blueberry Scones Recipe

Serving: 8 | Prep: | Cook: 20mins | Ready in:

Ingredients

- 2 cups flour
- 3 tbsp. sugar
- 2 1/2 tsp baking powder
- 1/4 tsp nutmeg
- 1/8 tsp allspice
- 1/4 tsp salt
- 5 tbsp plus 1 tsp cold butter
- 3/4 cup fresh or frozen blueberries
- 1/2 cup buttermilk
- 1 egg

Direction

- Preheat oven 400*.
- Sift together dry ingredients.
- Cut in cold butter until it resembles coarse crumbs.
- Toss berries into dry ingredients to coat. If using frozen be very gentle as not to crush.
- Beat egg in separate bowl.
- Beat in buttermilk.
- Make well in the center of dry add buttermilk mixture.
- Combine until dough comes together again being gentle to keep from crushing the berries.
- Turn out on floured surface
- Flour top and pat into a thick round
- Cut into 8 wedges and place on ungreased baking sheet lined with parchment paper. Brush tops with a little cream which has a dash of vanilla added.
- Bake 20-25 minutes.

5. Buttery Cinnamon Brown Sugar Rolls Recipe

Serving: 8 | Prep: | Cook: 8mins | Ready in:

Ingredients

- 1 roll of Hungry Jack Flaky biscuits
- 1/2 cup brown sugar
- 2 tsp cinnamon
- 1/2 cup butter - melted

Direction

- Combine brown sugar and cinnamon sprinkle half in the bottom of a ten inch round cake pan.
- Lay biscuits over sugar mixture. Cut a couple in half if you need to fit them all in.
- Sprinkle the other half of the sugar mixture over the biscuits.
- Pour melted butter over all.
- Bake at 350 degrees for about 8 to 10 minutes

6. Cheddar And Onion Scones Recipe

Serving: 8 | Prep: | Cook: 15mins | Ready in:

Ingredients

- 2 Cups all-purpose flour
- 2 Tbsp. finely chopped green onion
- 1 tsp. baking powder
- 1/4 tsp. baking soda
- 1/4 tsp. salt
- 1/4 tsp pepper
- 1 egg beaten
- 4 oz. shredded sharp cheddar cheese
- 1/2 Cup buttermilk or sour milk

Direction

- Preheat oven to 400 degrees. In a medium bowl combine flour, green onion, baking powder, baking soda, salt, and pepper. Make a well in the center of flour mixture, set aside.
- In a small bowl stir together egg, cheese, and buttermilk, Add egg mixture all at once to flour mixture. Using fork stir just until moistened.
- Turn dough out onto a lightly floured surface. Knead dough by folding and gently pressing dough for 10-12 strokes or until dough is nearly smooth. Divide dough in half. Pat or lightly roll half of the dough into a 5-inch circle. Cut into six wedges. Repeat with remaining dough. Place wedges 1 inch apart on an ungreased baking sheet.
- Bake scones for 15-18 minutes or until golden. Serve warm.

7. Cheese Fondue With Crusty Rolls Recipe

Serving: 8 | Prep: | Cook: 30mins | Ready in:

Ingredients

- Rhodes Warm-N-Serv™ Crusty rolls, or Sour Dough rolls baked following instructions
- 1 1/4 cups apple cider
- 3/4 pound gruyere cheese, grated
- 1/4 pound emmentaler cheese, grated
- 1 tablespoon cornstarch
- 1/2 teaspoon nutmeg
- 1/2 teaspoon dry mustard

Direction

- Cut baked crusty rolls into bite size pieces and set aside. In a fondue pot over medium heat or in a heavy sauce pan bring apple cider to a simmer; do not boil. Mix remaining ingredients together. While stirring with a wooden spoon, add cheese mixture a little at a time. Turn heat to low and continue stirring until the cheese is melted and mixture is smooth and glossy. Turn heat to lowest setting. Dip crusty roll cubes into the fondue.

8. Chocolate Chip Scones Recipe

Serving: 8 | Prep: | Cook: 35mins | Ready in:

Ingredients

- 2 cups flour
- 2 tsp baking powder
- 1/2 cup sugar
- 1/2 tsp salt
- 1/3 cup butter, cold cubes
- 2 eggs
- 1/3 cup Cream + a little more if the mix is too dry
- 1 cup light and dark chocolate chunks mixed. (I use Valrhona chocolate.)
- 1 egg, beaten - for wash

Direction

- Sift all the flour, baking powder, sugar, and salt into a large bowl. Then cut the cold butter into cubes and mix into the dry ingredients

with your hands. Mix until the butter is about pea size balls. Add the eggs one at a time and mix them in thoroughly. Then add the cream and chocolate and mix well. The dough will be wet.
- Line a baking sheet with parchment paper or spray with cooking spray to make sure the scones will not stick. Shape the dough into a large disc and pat it out to about 1/2 thick and score it into 6 or 8 pieces.
- Egg wash over the scones and bake at 375 F for about 35 minutes or until golden brown and baked through. Remove the scones from the oven and let cool. When cool, cut where you scored it, serve and enjoy.

9. Cinnamon Apple Raisin Bread Recipe

Serving: 8 | Prep: | Cook: 50mins | Ready in:

Ingredients

- 2 eggs
- 1 c sugar
- 1/2 c oil
- 1 t vanilla
- 1-1/2 c all-purpose flour
- 1 t baking powder
- 1/2 t baking soda
- 1/8 t salt
- 2 t cinnamon
- 1 c chopped, peeled apples
- 1/2 c raisins
- 1/2 c walnuts

Direction

- Grease a 9x5-inch loaf pan. In a large bowl combine all of the ingredients. Pour into the prepared pan. Bake in a preheated 350F oven for 50 to 60 minutes.

10. Cinnamon Jam Donut Muffins Recipe

Serving: 12 | Prep: | Cook: 10mins | Ready in:

Ingredients

- 2 Cups self raising flour
- 1/2 Cup brown sugar
- 60g unsalted butter, melted
- 2 eggs, lightly beaten
- 1 Cup buttermilk
- 1/4 Cup raspberry jam (or your favourite flavor)
- 2 Tbsp caster sugar
- 3 Tbsp unsalted butter, melted, extra
- 1/3 Cups caster sugar, extra
- 3 tsp ground cinnamon

Direction

- Preheat your oven to 350 degrees and spray a muffin tray with oil.
- Sift together self-raising flour & brown sugar. In another bowl mix together butter, eggs & buttermilk. Make a well in the dry ingredients and pour in the wet ingredients, mix until just combined (don't overmix).
- Microwave jam along with caster sugar for about 45 seconds, or until jam has melted and sugar is dissolved, mix thoroughly.
- Half fill muffin holes with muffin mixture and add a little bit of jam before filling up with more muffin mixture. Cook for 8 minutes in oven, until a skewer comes out clean.
- Melt extra butter and mix together extra caster sugar & cinnamon in another bowl. One by one, brush each muffin all over with butter and roll in cinnamon sugar mixture.

11. Cinnamon Raisin Scones Recipe

Serving: 12 | Prep: | Cook: 13mins | Ready in:

Ingredients

- 1 3/4 cups all-purpose flour
- 1/3 cup packed brown sugar
- 4 teaspoons baking powder
- 1 teaspoon ground cinnamon
- 1/3 cup margarine or butter
- 2 1/2 cups Stater Bros
- honey oats & Flakes cereal crushed to 1 3/4 cups
- 2 eggs beaten
- 1/2 cup buttermilk
- 1/2 cup raisins
- 1 egg beaten with 1 teaspoon water

Direction

- Preheat oven to 400F.
- Grease baking sheet.
- Combine flour, sugar, baking powder and cinnamon in large bowl.
- Cut in margarine until mixture forms coarse crumbs.
- Add cereal; mix well.
- Combine two eggs, buttermilk, and raisins in separate bowl; add to cereal mixture and stir until dough clings together.
- Knead on lightly floured surface 5 to 6 strokes.
- Divide dough in half.
- Roll or pat each half into a 6-inch circle, 3/4-inch thick.
- Cut each circle into 6 wedges.
- Separate and place on prepared baking sheet.
- Brush tops with egg and water mixture.
- Bake 11 to 13 minutes or until golden brown.

12. Cinnamon Roll Bites Recipe

Serving: 8 | Prep: | Cook: 10mins | Ready in:

Ingredients

- 1
- 1(12.4-oz)can Pillsbury Refrigerated orange Danish cinnamon rolls with icing

Direction

- Heat oven to 375°.
- Line a large cookie sheet with parchment paper.
- Cut each roll into 4 equal parts; place separately on the cookie sheet.
- Bake in preheated oven for 10 minutes.
- Uncover the icing cup; and microwave for 10 seconds.
- Drizzle icing overall and serve.
- (Makes 32 "bites")

13. Cinnamony Carrot Pumpkin Sweet Potato Bread Recipe

Serving: 0 | Prep: | Cook: 60mins | Ready in:

Ingredients

- 1 1/2 cup all-purpose flour
- 1/2 teaspoon salt
- 1/2 cup white sugar
- 1 t. baking soda
- 1 cup carrot, pumpkin, sweet potato or butternut squash puree
- 1/2 cup canola oil
- 2 large eggs, beaten
- 1/2 cup brown sugar
- 1/4 cup water
- 1 1/2 teaspoon cinnamon
- 1/2 teaspoon vanilla extract

Direction

- Preheat oven to 350.
- Whisk together flour salt, white sugar and baking soda.
- In separate bowl, mix together puree of choice, oil, eggs, brown sugar, water, cinnamon and vanilla extract. When well mixed, add dry mixture, mixing only to combine.
- Pour batter into greased 9x5 loaf pan. Bake 45-60 minutes or until tester comes out clean. Cool 10 minutes on rack; remove from pan.

14. Coconut Almond Bread Pudding Recipe

Serving: 6 | Prep: | Cook: 70mins | Ready in:

Ingredients

- 1 pan Rhodes™ Warm-N-Serv Buttery dinner rolls or Sticky buns
- 1/2 cup coconut, divided
- 1/2 cup chopped almonds, divided
- 3 eggs
- 1 teaspoon vanilla
- 1 teaspoon almond extract
- 1 pint whipping cream or 2 cups milk
- 3/4 cup sugar
- caramel topping, if desired

Direction

- Allow rolls to thaw enough that you can cut each one into 8 equal pieces to make 1-inch cubes.
- Place half of the roll cubes in the bottom of a sprayed 9x9-inch baking pan.
- Sprinkle with half of the coconut and half of the almonds.
- Repeat with remaining roll cubes, coconut and almonds.
- If any of the sticky glaze remains in the pan, scrap it out and place on top of roll cubes.
- In a bowl, combine the remaining ingredients and mix well.
- Pour mixture evenly over roll cubes.
- Cover and refrigerate at least one hour.
- Remove cover and bake at 350°F 50-60 minutes (cover with foil last 15 minutes of baking to prevent over browning).
- Serve warm, drizzled with caramel topping, if desired.

15. De Lish Bagel Bites Recipe

Serving: 1 | Prep: | Cook: 11mins | Ready in:

Ingredients

- - 1 bagel, plain or your choice (Double the ingredients for two people and so on)
- - 1/4 cup of bread Dipping oil of your flavour. Make sure it's oil based. (I suggest a garlic and parm mix, although works with vinegarette types)
- - steak seasoning, optional.

Direction

- Turn the oven on to 400 and allow to warm. For prep pull out a bowl, a baking sheet and a fork, plus all the ingredients.
- Tear the bagel into bite size pieces and place in the bowl one half at a time.
- Shake the bread dip to mix the ingredients around. That should be obvious.
- Pour half of the bread dip over the bagel pieces and then stir them around in order to cover some of the pieces more. They shouldn't be soaked, but coated lightly. Probably a good idea to use the fork so that your hands don't get greasy.
- Repeat that for the other half of the bagel. If 1/4 cup is not enough, feel free to use more, it won't ruin them. Just don't soak them, you don't want them soggy.
- When they're coated, place them on the baking sheet in one layer.
- Sprinkle the steak mix over the pieces and allow the oil to hold the seasoning. This step is optional, but adds more flavour.
- When the oven is heated, place the baking sheet on the middle rack and leave for 6 minutes.
- After the 6, pull out the sheet and move them around to prevent sticking and burning. Place inside for another 5.
- When times up, take them out and check for crisp-ness. They should be crunchy, not soggy.
- Place on plate, in bowl, or eat straight off the pan for few dishes.

- Enjoy.

16. Donut Muffins Recipe

Serving: 20 | Prep: | Cook: 20mins | Ready in:

Ingredients

- Muffins:
- 1 3/4 cup flour
- 1 1/2 tsp baking powder
- 1/2 tsp salt
- 1/2 tsp nutmeg (1/4 tsp if using freshly grated)
- 1/3 cup canola oil
- 3/4 cup sugar
- 1 egg
- 3/4 cup milk - lowfat is fine
- Toppings:
- 1/2 cup melted butter
- 1 tsp cinnamon
- 1/2 cup sugar
- OR/AND
- 1/2 cup confectioners sugar
- 2 tsp milk
- 1/4 tsp vanilla bean paste (or extract)

Direction

- In a bowl combine the flour, baking powder, salt, nutmeg and cinnamon.
- In a second bowl, combine the oil, sugar, egg and milk.
- Add the liquid ingredients to the dry and mix only to combine.
- Pour into greased muffin tins and bake at 350' for 12-15 minutes (20-25 if making large ones)
- While muffins bake, prepare topping of choice.
- For Cinnamon Sugar Topping:
- Mix together the sugar and cinnamon.
- Turn the muffins out immediately and while hot, dip the tops in the melted butter and then in the cinnamon sugar.
- For Glaze:
- Combine confectioners' sugar, vanilla, and milk and mix well. When muffins are cool, cover muffin tops with glaze.

17. Easy Caramel Sticky Buns Recipe

Serving: 12 | Prep: | Cook: 30mins | Ready in:

Ingredients

- Topping
- 1/4 cup melted butter
- 1/4 cup brown sugar
- 2 tbsp light corn syrup
- 1/4 cup chopped pecans
- buns
- 1 tbsp sugar
- 1/2 tsp cinnamon
- 1 can refrigerated biscuits

Direction

- Heat oven to 375.
- Grease 12 muffin cups.
- Combine topping ingredients and mix well.
- Spoon scant tbsp. of topping in each greased muffin cup.
- Combine sugar and cinnamon in medium size bowl.
- Separate biscuits into ten biscuits, then cut each biscuit into 6 pieces.
- Then toss the biscuit pieces in cinnamon sugar combo.
- Place 5 pieces of biscuit in each muffin cup, set on foil or cookie sheet to catch possible spills.
- Bake at 375 for 15-20 min or until golden.
- Cool for 1 min and then invert onto wax paper.
- Don't over bake and serve warm!
- Enjoy!!

18. Easy Donuts Recipe

Serving: 4 | Prep: | Cook: 1mins | Ready in:

Ingredients

- 2 packages refrigerated buttermilk biscuits, small 7.5 oz
- 5 cups vegetable oil (for frying)

Direction

- Pre-heat oil in a skillet or electric fryer to 365 degrees
- Open biscuit package, round the edges of biscuits and poke a hole in each one. Let biscuits lay in a tray or plate.
- Place biscuits one by one in hot oil. Use tongs or skewers to check the color of the underside of each biscuit and turn when they reach the desired golden brown color (approx. 35 to 45 seconds). Check the bottom again and remove donuts when they are evenly brown on each side.
- .
- FROSTINGS:
- .
- Powdered sugar
- Sprinkles
- Chocolate frosting
- Jams, jellies
- Peanut butter
- Cream cheese
- Sugar and cinnamon
- Use your imagination!

19. Easy Lemonade Scones Recipe

Serving: 8 | Prep: | Cook: 15mins | Ready in:

Ingredients

- 10 ounces cream
- 10 ounces lemonade
- 4 cups self-rising flour

Direction

- Preheat oven to 425F.
- Mix sifted flour, cream, and lemonade with a knife to a consistent dough.
- If it is too dry, add more cream.
- If it is too wet, add more flour.
- Place dough onto a lightly floured surface.
- Shape into balls, coat in flour, and place on baking tray.
- Bake at 425F for 10-15 minutes or until tops turn golden.
- Allow to cool on a wire rack.
- Serve with whipped cream and boysenberry jam.

20. Easy Raisin Bran Quick Bread Recipe

Serving: 12 | Prep: | Cook: 50mins | Ready in:

Ingredients

- 2 cups Raisin Bran cereal, divided
- 1-1/4 cups milk
- 1/4 cup margarine, melted, divided
- 1 egg
- 3/4 cup sugar
- 2 cups flour
- 1 Tbsp. baking powder
- 1 tsp. ground cinnamon
- 1 Tbsp. sugar

Direction

- Preheat oven to 350°F. Spray 9 x 5-inch loaf pan with cooking spray.
- Mix 1-1/2 cups of the cereal, the milk and 2 Tbsp. of the margarine in medium bowl. Let stand 1 minute. Add egg and 3/4 cup sugar; mix well. Stir in flour, baking powder and cinnamon until well blended. Spread into prepared loaf pan.
- Mix remaining 1/2 cup cereal, remaining 2 Tbsp. margarine and 1 Tbsp. sugar until well

blended; sprinkle over batter. Gently press cereal mixture into batter.
- Bake 50 minutes or until toothpick inserted in center comes out clean. Cool 10 minutes in pan on wire rack; remove bread from pan. Cool completely.

21. Fluffy Easy Donuts Surprise Recipe

Serving: 56 | Prep: | Cook: 5mins | Ready in:

Ingredients

- 1 (18.25 oz.) package moist cake mix, any flavor
- 1/2 C. flour
- 4 eggs
- 1 1/4 C. water
- 3 C. oil for frying, or as needed
- 1/4 C. confectioners' sugar for dusting

Direction

- In a large bowl, combine the cake mix, flour, water, and eggs. Beat with an electric mixer on low speed for 5 minutes, or until batter is free of lumps. Heat oil in a large, deep skillet until it reaches 375 degrees F (190 degrees C). Using a small scoop equal to about 2 Tbs., carefully drop batter into hot oil in batches so as not to overcrowd. Cook donuts in hot oil for 5 minutes, or until golden brown, flipping once with a fork mid-way through for even cooking. Carefully remove donuts from oil with slotted spoon or tongs, and drain on paper towels. Dust with confectioners' sugar before serving.
- Makes 56 servings.

22. French Toast Recipe

Serving: 10 | Prep: | Cook: 25mins | Ready in:

Ingredients

- 3 pcs. eggs, slightly beaten
- 1 tbsp. sugar
- one and one-fourth cups skim milk
- one half tsp. vanilla extract
- 10 slices white / whole wheat bread
- oil

Direction

- In a bowl, combine eggs, sugar, milk and vanilla. Mix well. Soak bread slices in mixture.
- Heat a non-stick pan and add 1 tbsp. oil. Cook both sides of bread until golden brown.
- Place on serving platter and keep warm.
- Can be served with syrup or vanilla yoghurt.

23. Isaiahs Toaster Grilled Cheese Recipe

Serving: 1 | Prep: | Cook: | Ready in:

Ingredients

- 2 slices of bread
- little kid size handful of shredded cheese my kids like "Kraft" Mozza-Cheddar shredded cheese
- enough butter for both bread slices or omit it because toasters varey.

Direction

- With our toaster it can cook the toasted cheese without the butter so without the butter.
- Place cheese on one slice of bread, and put both slices together and put into toaster, we have ours set to medium and a half.
- Wait for it to pop up and presto toasted cheese quicker than the pan.

- Or with butter, just butter both slices and but cheese on one bread slice and put together.
- Put into toaster and wait to pop up and enjoy!
- Very kid friendly.

24. Lazy Maple Sticky Buns Recipe

Serving: 1 | Prep: | Cook: 18mins | Ready in:

Ingredients

- 1/4 cup packed brown sugar
- 1/4 cup butter
- 2 Tbsp. pure maple syrup
- 1/4 cup chopped pecans
- 1 (8-oz.) can refrig. cresent rolls
- 1 Tbsp. granulated sugar
- 1/2 tsp. ground cinnamon

Direction

- Remove dough from package (don't unroll dough).
- Cut roll into 12 slices.
- Combine granulated sugar and cinnamon.
- Dip both side of each slice of dough into sugar mixture.
- Arrange slices in prepared pan, cut side down.
- Combine other ingredients to make 2nd sugar mixture.
- Sprinkle this over the top of the rolls.
- Bake at 375 degrees for 18 minutes or until golden.
- Invert pan immediately onto a serving platter.
- Serve immediately.

25. Lemon Verbena Scones Recipe

Serving: 9 | Prep: | Cook: 20mins | Ready in:

Ingredients

- 2 cups all purpose flour
- 1 1/2 cups rolled oats (I blenderize to a powder)
- 2 tsp. baking powder
- 1/2 tsp. baking soda
- 1/2 tsp. salt
- 1/4 cup brown sugar
- 1/4 cup cold butter
- 1/4 cup finely chopped fresh lemon verbena leaves
- 1 egg, beaten
- 1/2 cup plain yogurt
- 1/4 cup milk

Direction

- Preheat oven to 425° F.
- In a large bowl, combine flour, oats, baking powder, baking soda, salt, and brown sugar.
- Cut in the butter with your fingers or a pastry cutter until the mixture resembles coarse crumbs.
- Add the lemon verbena leaves; mix until combined just combined.
- Make a well in the center of flour mixture.
- Add the egg, yogurt, and milk, stirring well.
- Mix in with the flour mixture to form a soft dough.
- Coat a12-inch cast iron skillet with a non-stick cooking spray.
- With floured hands, pat the dough into skillet.
- Cut with a sharp, serrated knife into eight wedges. (You can also pat the dough into a circle this same size on a baking sheet, and then cut into wedges.)
- Bake at 425° F for 15 minutes, or until lightly browned.

26. MUFFINS THAT TASTE LIKE DONUTS Recipe

Serving: 8 | Prep: | Cook: 20mins | Ready in:

Ingredients

- In a large bowl, combine:

- 1 3/4 c. flour
- 1 1/2 tsp. baking powder
- 1/2 tsp. salt
- 1/2 tsp. nutmeg
- 1/4 tsp. cinnamon
- In another bowl, combine:
- 1 egg
- 1/3 c. oil
- 3/4 c. sugar
- 3/4 c. milk

Direction

- Add wet ingredients to dry, and stir only to combine (do not overmix!). Fill muffin tins 2/3 full and bake at 350 for 20-25 minutes.
- Meanwhile, melt 1/2 cup margarine or butter and set aside.
- Combine 3/4 cup sugar and 1 tsp. cinnamon in another bowl and set aside.
- Take muffins out, and while they're still hot, dip in melted margarine and then in cinnamon sugar mixture.

27. Maple Oatmeal Scones Recipe

Serving: 14 | Prep: | Cook: 25mins | Ready in:

Ingredients

- 3 1/2 c. AP flour
- 1 c. WW flour
- 1 c. quick cooking oats
- 2 T. baking powder
- 2 T. sugar
- 2 t. salt
- 1 pound cold unsalted butter diced
- 1/2 c. cold buttermilk
- 1/2 c. maple syrup
- 4 extra large eggs lightly beaten
- 1 egg beaten with 1 T. water for egg wash
- glaze
- 1 1/4 c. confectioners sugar
- 1/2 c. maple syrup
- 1 t. vanilla

Direction

- Preheat oven to 400
- In mixing bowl combine flour, oats, baking powder, sugar, and salt
- Blend the butter in at lowest speed until it is in pea sized pieces
- In a bowl combine buttermilk, eggs and maple syrup
- Add quickly to flour mixture
- Mix till just blended
- Dump onto floured surface
- Roll the dough 1in. thick, you should see lumps of butter in the dough
- Cut in 3in. rounds
- Brush with egg wash
- Bake 25 min.
- Mix glaze ingredients
- When scones are cool drizzle with glaze

28. Mini Crescent Cinnamon Rolls Recipe

Serving: 4 | Prep: | Cook: 17mins | Ready in:

Ingredients

- 1 can refrigerated crescent dinner rolls
- 1/4 cup butter, softened
- 4 teaspoons granulated sugar
- 2 teaspoons ground cinnamon
- 1/4 cup finely chopped pecans (or raisins, chopped)
- Prepared cream cheese or vanilla frosting or powdered sugar glaze (1/2 cup powdered sugar and 1 Tblsp. milk)

Direction

- Heat oven to 375°F.
- Unroll dough; separate dough into 4 rectangles. Firmly press perforations to seal.
- Spread 1 tablespoon butter evenly over each dough rectangle. In small bowl, mix granulated sugar and cinnamon. Sprinkle

evenly over rectangles. Sprinkle each with nuts or raisins. Starting with short side of each rectangle, roll up; pinch edges to seal. (Mine didn't want to seal because I put the sugar edge to edge I guess, but I didn't worry about pinching the seams and they were still perfect.)
- With serrated knife, cut each roll into 5 slices (or use a piece of dental floss to wrap around each roll and cut into 5 pieces. Place slices, cut side down, in ungreased 8- or 9-inch square pan.
- Bake 17 to 23 minutes or until golden brown. Cool 5 minutes.
- Heat frosting in microwave and drizzle over warm rolls.

29. Oatmeal Raisin Quick Bread Recipe

Serving: 0 | Prep: | Cook: 80mins | Ready in:

Ingredients

- 1 & 1/4 cup buttermilk
- 1/2 cup regular (old-fashioned) uncooked oatmeal
- 1 & 1/2 cup all-purpose flour
- 1 teaspoon ground cinnamon
- 1 teaspoon ground ginger
- 1 teaspoon baking soda
- 1 teaspoon baking powder
- 1/2 teaspoon salt
- 1/2 cup packed light brown sugar
- 1/2 cup unsalted butter, melted
- 2 large eggs
- 1/2 cup mixed jumbo raisins (or golden raisins)

Direction

- In a large mixing bowl, combine buttermilk and uncooked oatmeal; stir thoroughly and allow mixture to stand for at least 30 minutes, stirring occasionally. When time has elapsed, preheat oven to 350 degrees F; grease and flour a standard-size loaf pan. In smaller bowl, combine flour, cinnamon, ginger, baking soda, baking powder and salt; set aside. Add brown sugar, butter, eggs and raisins to the buttermilk/oatmeal mixture and beat using an electric mixer until thoroughly combined. Next, add the dry ingredients to the wet, stirring by hand until blended. Pour batter into prepared loaf pan and bake at 350 degrees F for approximately 55-65 minutes, or until a toothpick inserted in the center of loaf comes out clean. When bread is done, remove pan from oven and allow loaf to cool in pan for about 10 minutes, then turn out onto a wire rack to cool completely.
- Serve at room temperature plain or with sweet orange marmalade, berry jam, butter, softened cream cheese or honey. Store leftovers airtight to enjoy later.

30. Oatmeal Scones Recipe

Serving: 18 | Prep: | Cook: 16mins | Ready in:

Ingredients

- 1 2/3 cups all-purpose flour
- 1/3 cup plus 2 tablespoons packed light brown sugar
- 3/4 teaspoon cinnamon
- 1 tablespoon baking powder
- 3/4 teaspoon baking soda
- 1/2 teaspoon salt
- 1 1/3 cups plus 2 tablespoons old-fashioned rolled oats
- 1 1/2 sticks (3/4 cup) cold unsalted butter, cut into tablespoon pieces
- 2/3 cup well-shaken buttermilk plus additional for brushing

Direction

- Put oven rack in middle position and preheat oven to 425°F.

- Sift together flour, 1/4 cup brown sugar, cinnamon, baking powder, baking soda, and salt into a food processor. Add 1 1/3 cups oats and pulse 15 times. Add butter and pulse until mixture resembles coarse meal with some pea-size lumps. Transfer to a bowl.
- Add buttermilk and stir with a fork until a dough just forms. Gently knead on a floured surface 6 times.
- Pat into a 9-inch square (1/2 inch thick). Cut into 9 (3-inch) squares. Cut each square diagonally to form 2 triangles. Transfer to an ungreased baking sheet.
- Brush with buttermilk and sprinkle with remaining brown sugar and oats. Bake until golden brown, about 16 minutes.

31. One Bowl Banana Bread Recipe

Serving: 10 | Prep: | Cook: 2hours1mins | Ready in:

Ingredients

- 3-4 ripe bananas
- 1/2 cup butter or margarine-melted
- 3/4 cup brown sugar
- 2 eggs
- 1 tsp vanilla
- 2 cups flour
- 1 tsp baking soda
- 1/4 tsp salt
- 1/4 tsp cinnamon (optional)
- pinch of nutmeg (optional, but nutmeg and bananas are best friends :)
- Optional add-ins:
- 1/3 cup chocolate chips or nuts
- ~For chocolate banana Bread~
- Replace 1/4 cup of flour with unsweetened cocoa powder. (no more or the loaf won't hold together)

Direction

- Preheat the oven to 350F, and lightly grease a 9x5" or 8x4" loaf pan (I only use glass).
- In a large bowl mash the bananas with a fork, and make a well in the center of the mashed bananas (pushing the bananas up the sides of the bowl). Add the brown sugar and melted butter in the well and stir to combine. Add in the eggs and vanilla and mix with the sugar and butter. Then incorporate the bananas without over mixing.
- Place a sieve over the bowl and sift in the flour, baking soda, salt and spices. If you're adding chocolate chips or nuts, add them in now.
- Fold together until it's just combined. Pour batter into the loaf pan and bake for 45-60 minutes, until a toothpick inserted in the center comes out clean. (The more banana you use the more moist it is and may take up to 65 mins to bake at times, but check on it early just in case).
- Let cool for at least 30 minutes before cutting into, if you can.
- ~For Muffins, grease a 12 cup muffin tin and bake for 20-25 minutes.

32. Orange Praline Quick Bread Recipe

Serving: 0 | Prep: | Cook: 60mins | Ready in:

Ingredients

- 2 cups all-purpose flour
- 2 teaspoons baking powder
- 1/2 teaspoon baking soda
- 1/2 teaspoon salt
- 1 cup sugar
- 1 cup sour cream
- 1/2 cup Land O Lakes® butter, softened
- 2 Land O Lakes® All-Natrual eggs
- 1 tablespoon freshly grated orange peel
- 1 teaspoon vanilla
- 1 cup chopped pecans
- glaze
- 1/3 cup firmly packed brown sugar

- 1/3 cup Land O Lakes® butter
- 1/4 cup finely chopped pecans

Direction

- Heat oven to 350°F. Combine flour, baking powder, baking soda and salt in small bowl. Set aside.
- Combine all remaining bread ingredients, except pecans, in large bowl. Beat at medium speed, scraping bowl often, until well mixed. Reduce speed to low. Beat, gradually adding flour mixture, just until moistened. Stir in 1 cup pecans.
- Spoon batter evenly into 4 greased (5 1/2x3-inch) mini loaf pans. Bake for 30 to 35 minutes or until toothpick inserted in center comes out clean. Cool 10 minutes; remove from pans.
- Meanwhile, combine brown sugar and 1/3 cup butter in 1-quart saucepan. Cook over medium heat until mixture comes to a boil (3 to 4 minutes). Spoon glaze mixture over warm loaves. Immediately sprinkle with 1/4 cup pecans.
- Recipe Tip
- - Substitute 1 greased (9x5-inch) loaf pan. Bake for 60 to 65 minutes.
- - Serve bread with maple-flavored butter. Combine 1/3 cup softened butter, 1/4 cup Florida Sunshine Marmalade and 1 tablespoon maple syrup in small bowl; mix well.

33. Peachy Cinnamon Rolls Recipe

Serving: 6 | Prep: | Cook: 25mins | Ready in:

Ingredients

- 6 frozen cinnamon rolls, thawed (ex Rhodes brand)
- 21 oz can peach pie filling
- whipped cream, if desired

Direction

- Remove rolls from the pan they come in and cut each roll into 4 equal pieces and set aside.
- Spray pan with non-stick cooking spray.
- Spread pie filling evenly in the bottom of the sprayed pan.
- Drop the cinnamon roll pieces on top of the pie filling to cover evenly.
- Bake at 350°F 25-30 minutes.
- Serve warm with whipped cream, if desired.

34. Port Elizabeth Scones Recipe

Serving: 6 | Prep: | Cook: 15mins | Ready in:

Ingredients

- 2 c flour
- 2/3 c butter
- 1 tbsp baking powder
- 1/4 tsp salt
- 1/4 c sugar
- 2/3 c slightly beaten eggs
- 1/2 c grated jack cheese
- 1/2 c apricot jam
- butter to spread on scones

Direction

- Cut 2/3 c butter into flour, baking powder, sugar, and salt.
- Add eggs.
- Mixture will be moist.
- Knead lightly-10-12 times.
- Pat out into a rectangle1 inch thick on lightly floured surface
- Cut into 2 inch circles with cutter
- Bake on greased baking sheet at 425degrees for about 15 minutes until golden brown.
- Split open while still hot.
- Butter each half and then spread with jam.
- Top each half next with cheese and serve warm.
- Makes about 12 halves.

35. Pumpkin Beer Quick Bread Recipe From Lv Anderson Recipe

Serving: 12 | Prep: | Cook: 1hours15mins | Ready in:

Ingredients

- Oil or butter for greasing the pan
- 1¼ cup all-purpose flour
- ½ cup whole-wheat flour
- 1 teaspoon baking powder
- ½ teaspoon baking soda
- ½ teaspoon salt
- 1½ teaspoons ground cinnamon
- ½ teaspoon ground ginger
- Pinch ground nutmeg
- Pinch ground allspice
- 3 tablespoons unsalted butter
- 1 cup pumpkin purée
- 1 cup brown sugar
- 2 large eggs
- 1 cup pumpkin ale

Direction

- 1. Heat the oven to 350°F. Grease a 9-inch loaf pan. Combine the flours, baking powder, baking soda, salt, cinnamon, ginger, nutmeg, and allspice in a large bowl.
- 2. Melt the butter in a medium saucepan over low heat (or in a medium bowl in the microwave). Remove from the heat. Stir in the pumpkin and brown sugar, then stir in the eggs. Finally, stir in the pumpkin ale. Add the pumpkin mixture to the dry ingredients and stir just until combined, then transfer the batter to the greased pan.
- 3. Bake until a toothpick inserted into the center of the loaf comes out clean, about 1 hour. Cool thoroughly, then slice and serve. (Leftover pumpkin bread can be wrapped in foil or plastic wrap and stored at room temperature for up to a few days.)

36. Pumpkin Walnut Breakfast Bread Recipe

Serving: 12 | Prep: | Cook: 32mins | Ready in:

Ingredients

- 1/2 cup canola oil
- 1 cup sugar
- 1/2 cup plus 2 tablespoons molasses
- 3 large eggs
- 1 15-ounce can pure pumpkin
- 1/2 cuo buttermilk
- 2 3/4 cups all purpose flour
- 1 1/2 teaspoon baking soda
- 1 teaspoon salt
- 2 teaspoons ground ginger
- 1 teaspoon cinnamon
- 1/4 teaspoon ground cloves
- 1 cup medium chopped walnuts

Direction

- Combine flour, salt, baking soda and spices and set aside.
- With an electric mixer beat together oil, sugar, molasses and eggs until smooth.
- Add the pumpkin and beat until well blended.
- Alternately add the flour and butter until smooth.
- Stir in chopped walnuts.
- Pour into 2 oiled standard size bread pans.
- Bake at 350 for 30-36 minutes or until a toothpick inserted into the middle comes out clean.
- Cool completely before removing from pans.

37. Quick Donuts Recipe

Serving: 0 | Prep: | Cook: | Ready in:

Ingredients

- 1 or more can of sweet milk biscuits
- cooking oil to deep fry

Direction

- Punch holes with finger or use donut cutter to cut hole in each biscuit.
- Then stretch each hole of biscuit, drop in hot fat and cook on each side until desired brownness.
- Place on brown paper bag.
- Immediately sprinkle with sugar and serve with hot coffee to adults or hot chocolate or milk to children.

38. Quick Raisin Bread Pudding Recipe

Serving: 0 | Prep: | Cook: 15mins | Ready in:

Ingredients

- 3 slices raisin bread
- butter or margarine
- 3 eggs
- 1/2 tsp. vanilla
- 13 oz. evaporated milk
- 1/3 c. sugar

Direction

- Toast bread and spread with butter.
- Cut bread into 1/2 inch cubes and divide among six 6 oz. custard cups.
- Combine eggs, sugar and vanilla.
- Stir in milk and 1 cup boiling water.
- Pour mixture over toast.
- Place custard cups in electric skillet; fill with hot water to within 1/2 inch of top of cups.
- Over high heat, heat water just to boiling.
- Reduce heat to low, cover and simmer 15 minutes or until knife inserted in center comes out clean.
- Cool 15 minutes on wire rack.
- Serve warm or cold.

- ===
- Note: pat2me--Thinks it could be put in a greased casserole dish in the oven.
- momo_55grandma--(Suggestion) Put the raisin bread in bottom of greased casserole dish whip rest of ingredients together pour over it bake 30 minutes at 350 degrees with lid on casserole.

39. Quick And Easy Donuts Recipe

Serving: 10 | Prep: | Cook: 10mins | Ready in:

Ingredients

- 1 can refrigerated biscuits
- 1 cup cinnamon sugar mix
- or
- 1 cup powdered sugar
- oil to fry

Direction

- Heat pan of oil on medium to high until very hot.
- Using a cutter or pop lid cut hole in center of biscuit.
- Fry in oil until brown, both sides.
- Roll in cinnamon and sugar mix, or powdered sugar.
- Makes 10 donuts and 10 holes.

40. Quick And Easy Scones Recipe

Serving: 6 | Prep: | Cook: 15mins | Ready in:

Ingredients

- 3 cups self raising flour
- 1 tbsp icing sugar
- pinch salt
- 60g soft butter

- 1 1/4 cups your favourite milk
- jams and cream to serve

Direction

- Mix flour with salt and icing sugar.
- Rub in butter, and then stir in milk.
- Knead lightly and press dough out to 2 cm thick. Cut out into rounds or rough squares- you choose.
- Place scones, almost touching, on a greased oven tray and brush with a little extra milk.
- Bake in a very hot oven for 15 mins.
- Serve warm and next time make a double batch!

41. Raisin Bread Recipe

Serving: 0 | Prep: | Cook: 4hours | Ready in:

Ingredients

- 2/3 cup plain yogourt
- 1 egg
- 1/4 cup margarine or butter
- 1/4 tsp salt
- 4 tbs molasses
- Pinch baking soda
- 1 1/2 tsp yeast
- 3/4 cup raisins
- 1 tsp cinnamon
- 1 tbs vital wheat gluten
- 1 cup whole wheat flour
- 1 cup bread flour
- 1 tsp of olive oil for the bowl

Direction

- Place everything but the raisins in the bowl of a KA and mix with the hook, or mix by hand.
- No, I do not proof the yeast.
- If using a KA you will need to scrape the inside of the bowl occasionally.
- Add additional flour if the dough is too wet, 1 tsp at a time.
- Knead for approx. 10 minutes. This dough will leave the sides and bottom of the bowl but will not remain that way.
- After kneading for 9 minutes, add the raisins.
- Rinse out your bowl and dry. Add the oil and swirl to coat the bottom of the bowl.
- Put the dough in and turn to coat. Cover with a tea towel.
- Place the bowl in a warm, draft free place to double. This will take anywhere from 1-2 hours, be patient.
- Dough is ready when you can make a 1/2 inch indentation, with two fingers, in the dough and the indentation remains.
- Lightly dust your work surface with about 1 tsp of flour. Turn dough out onto work surface and knead about 10 times.
- Form into a round loaf.
- Place dough on a parchment lined plate and loosely tent with plastic wrap.
- Place in a warm place to rise, about 30 minutes.
- Preheat oven 375°. If using a pizza stone, place it in the oven now. You can use a cookie tray as well but do not put that in the oven now.
- After 30 minutes slide the parchment and dough onto the pizza stone or cookie sheet.
- Bake for approx. 30 minutes or until the loaf sounds hollow when tapped.
- This recipe is loosely based on Welsh Bread form AR.

42. Snickerdoodle Banana Bread Recipe

Serving: 12 | Prep: | Cook: 1hours20mins | Ready in:

Ingredients

- 3/4 cup butter, softened
- 1/3 cup milk
- 2 cups sugar
- 4 eggs
- 4 bananas, mashed

- 4 cups flour
- 1 Tbsp. baking powder
- 1 tsp. baking soda
- 2 Tbsp. cinnamon
- 1/2 tsp. salt
- Topping*
- 1/2 cup sugar
- 1 tsp. cinnamon

Direction

- Heat the oven to 350 degrees F. Grease 2, 9 x 5-inch loaf pans. Mix your topping ingredients. Sprinkle generously all over the inside of the pans. Set the remaining topping aside.
- In a large bowl, whisk together the flour, baking powder, baking soda, cinnamon and salt.
- Beat the butter, milk and sugar. Add the eggs and the bananas. Stir this into the dry ingredients.
- Pour evenly into the loaf pans. Sprinkle with remaining topping. Bake for 1 hour.
- Cool in pans for 10 minutes. Turn onto a rack to cool completely.
- *Note: I made lots of extra topping. I think I tripled the recipe. Then, I would only put half the batter in the pans and sprinkle on some of the topping. Then, fill the pans with the remaining batter.

43. Sorta Quick Cinnamon Rolls Recipe

Serving: 8 | Prep: | Cook: 25mins | Ready in:

Ingredients

- 1 tablespoon unsalted butter, melted, for 9" round cake pan
- cinnamon sugar FILLING
- ¾ cup packed dark brown sugar
- ¼ cup granulated sugar
- 2 teaspoons cinnamon
- 1/8 teaspoon cloves
- 1/8 teaspoon salt
- 1 tablespoon unsalted butter, melted
- biscuit dough
- 2 ½ cups unbleached all-purpose flour, plus flour for work surface
- 2 tablespoons granulated sugar
- 1¼ teaspoons baking powder
- ½ teaspoon baking soda
- ½ teaspoon salt
- 1¼ cups buttermilk
- 6 tablespoons unsalted butter, melted
- icing
- 2 tablespoons cream cheese, softened
- 2 tablespoons buttermilk
- 1 cup powdered sugar

Direction

- Adjust oven rack to upper-middle position and heat oven to 425 degrees. Pour 1 tablespoon melted butter in 9-inch non-stick cake pan; brush to coat pan. Spray wire cooling rack with non-stick cooking spray; set aside.
- MAKE CINNAMON FILLING:
- Combine sugars, spices, and salt in small bowl.
- Add 1 tablespoon melted butter and stir with fork or fingers until mixture resembles wet sand; set filling mixture aside.
- MAKE BISCUIT DOUGH:
- Whisk flour, sugar, baking powder, baking soda, and salt in large bowl.
- Whisk buttermilk and 2 tablespoons melted butter in measuring cup or small bowl.
- Add liquid to dry ingredients and stir with wooden spoon until liquid is absorbed (dough will look very shaggy), about 30 seconds.
- Transfer dough to lightly floured work surface and knead until just smooth and no longer shaggy. Handle the dough as little as possible.
- Pat dough with hands into 12 by 9-inch rectangle.
- Pat filling within ½" of the edge of the rectangle. Roll the rectangle and pinch the seam closed. Turn seam side down.

- Cut into 8 pieces. Use a serrated knife or unflavored dental floss to cut biscuits.
- Arrange buns in buttered cake pan. Brush with 2 tablespoons remaining melted butter.
- Bake until edges are golden brown, 23 to 25 minutes.
- Use offset metal spatula to loosen buns from pan; without separating, slide buns out of pan onto greased cooling rack. Cool about 5 minutes before icing.
- MAKE ICING:
- While buns are cooling, line rimmed baking sheet with parchment paper (for easy clean-up); set rack with buns over baking sheet.
- Whisk cream cheese until softened. Add buttermilk and beat until thick and smooth (mixture will look like cottage cheese at first).
- Sift powdered sugar over; whisk until smooth glaze forms, about 30 seconds.
- Spoon glaze evenly over buns; serve immediately.
- NOTE: When cutting the rolls, I usually cut off about 1/2 inch at each end so that all the rolls have a lot of filling.

44. Strawberry Scones Recipe

Serving: 24 | Prep: | Cook: 12mins | Ready in:

Ingredients

- 3 cups all purpose, unbleached flour
- 1/2 cup sugar
- 2 1/2 teaspoons baking powder
- 1/2 teaspoon baking soda
- 3/4 teaspoon salt
- 1 1/2 sticks of cold, unsalted butter cut into tiny pieces
- 1 cup Half and Half
- 1 tablespoon plain yogurt
- 12 frozen strawberries, sliced

Direction

- Preheat oven to 425°.
- Sift the flour, baking powder, baking soda, salt, and sugar together. Add the cold pieces of butter and work it into the flour using your hands. Don't overwork the flour and butter. Mix the yogurt into the Half and Half and add the strawberries. Add the liquid to the flour and mix gently.
- Turn the dough out onto the lightly floured counter. Pat the dough into a square about 1/2 inch thick. Cut the dough into squares and place on a parchment covered cookie sheet. Bake for about 12 to 15 minutes or until golden brown.
- Allow to cool for 5 minutes and then glaze with a mixture of 1/2 cup powder sugar, 1/2 teaspoon vanilla, and a splash of Orange Juice.

45. Super Simple Scones Recipe

Serving: 8 | Prep: | Cook: 12mins | Ready in:

Ingredients

- 2 cups all-purpose flour (King Arthur preferred)
- 1 tablespoon baking powder
- 1/2 teaspoon salt
- 3 tablespoons sugar
- 1 1/4 cup heavy cream, plus more for brushing
- About 1/2 cup dried fruit, such as dried blueberries, apricots (cut into small pieces), or dried cranberries, or other fruits of your choice
- About 1/4 cup toasted nuts (I like sliced almonds, but pecans or walnuts work too) or to taste

Direction

- Heat oven to 425 degrees F. Lightly grease a baking pan.
- Sift together, in a medium bowl, the flour, baking powder and salt, stir in the sugar. Add the fruits and nuts. Stir with a fork to combine.
- Add the cream; stir just until a dough forms.

- Gather the dough into a ball; turn out onto a lightly floured counter or work surface, and fold and kneed about 6 or 7 times then pat out into about a 10 inch round about 1/2 inch thick. Cut with a knife or pastry cutter into 8 wedges. Place them on the prepared sheet; brush the tops with cream and sprinkle with some sugar; place in the oven (rack in the middle of the oven); and bake 12 to 15 minutes, or until nice and browned.

46. Vegan Bran Raisin Bread Recipe

Serving: 12 | Prep: | Cook: 60mins | Ready in:

Ingredients

- 2 tablespoons apple butter or fig puree
- 1 ¼ cup fat-free (preferably unsweetened) soy or almond milk
- 1 ½ cups Raisin Bran cereal
- 1/3 cup molasses
- ½ cup sultana raisins
- 1 teaspoon vanilla
- 1 cup whole wheat flour
- ½ cup all-purpose flour
- 1 tablespoon baking powder
- 1 teaspoon cinnamon
- ¼ cup ground cloves

Direction

- Heat oven to 350 degrees. Spray a 9-inch loaf pan with vegetable oil.
- Blend the fruit butter with soymilk, raisin bran, molasses, raisins and vanilla.
- Let mixture stand for a few minutes; it will turn mushy.
- Meanwhile, in a large bowl, combine the flours, baking powder cinnamon and cloves.
- Add the raisin bran mixture, and stir just until blended.
- Pour into the prepared pan and bake for about 1 hour.

47. Walnut And Cheddar Scones Recipe

Serving: 4 | Prep: | Cook: 20mins | Ready in:

Ingredients

- 2 cups all purpose flour
- 1 tsp baking powder
- 1 tsp baking soda
- 1 tsp fresh thyme, chopped (or ½ tsp dried)
- ¼ tsp salt
- ¼ tsp pepper
- 2/3 cup butter
- 1 cup old cheddar, grated
- 1/3 cup chopped walnuts
- 2 tbsp Italian parsley, finely chopped
- 1 clove garlic, minced
- ½ cup 10% cream

Direction

- Preheat oven to 400*F.
- Mix dry ingredients together, incorporating well.
- Rub the butter into this mixture until coarse and crumbly in texture.
- Add the cheese, parsley, walnuts, and garlic.
- Combine well.
- Drizzle the cream into the mixture, stirring well to make a soft dough.
- You may add more cream if necessary.
- Knead the dough gently on floured working surface for about 5 minutes.
- Pat out by hand to a disc of about 1 inch in thickness.
- Cut into 8 wedges.
- Place wedges on parchment paper lined baking sheet.
- Bake about 20 minutes until golden brown.
- To serve:
- Eat as is with butter, or add your favorite filling.

48. Bagel Sandwich Recipe

Serving: 2 | Prep: | Cook: 5mins | Ready in:

Ingredients

- two fresh bagels
- 1/2 cup of egg beaters
- 4 leaves of basil, or 2 tsp
- pinch of salt
- a few pinches of pepper
- 1/2 avocado
- soy bacon
- 1 tbsp parmesan cheese
- 2 slices of swiss cheese
- veganaise

Direction

- Heat a medium sized pan to medium heat.
- PAM/butter coat the pan lightly.
- Pour in egg so that it's about 1/4" in depth.
- Add salt and pepper.
- Tear up basil leaves into the egg.
- Sprinkle parmesan cheese on.
- Microwave frozen soy bacon (3 strips) for about 1 minute.
- Break each slice in 1/2 (making a total of 6 bacon pieces).
- Slice and toast the bagels.
- When the top of the egg is no longer shiny/watery/jiggly give it another 20-30 seconds.
- Turn off the heat, flip the egg over so it looks like an omelette.
- Slice the omelette in two.
- Lightly put veganaise on the bagels.
- Place egg on the bagel.
- Place Swiss cheese on top.
- Place 3 1/2 bacon strips on top.
- Place sliced avocado on top.
- Place top of bagel on top.
- Optionally:
- Baby bell peppers in the eggs
- Tomatoes in the eggs
- Sausage instead of bacon
- Whole wheat pita instead of bagel (in this case you would put the entire omelette inside a 1/2 pita)
- Stack the eggs and cheese onto one bagel for the ultimate breakfast!

49. Lemonade Scones Recipe

Serving: 6 | Prep: | Cook: 12mins | Ready in:

Ingredients

- 3 cups self raising flour
- 1 cup lemonade
- 1 cup cream

Direction

- Set oven to 200oc.mix all of the ingredients together and knead. Cut into rounds and cook for 10-15min.

50. Ooey Gooey Breakfast Bagel Recipe

Serving: 2 | Prep: | Cook: 10mins | Ready in:

Ingredients

- 1 bagel
- 2 T cream cheese
- 2 slices bacon
- 1 fried egg

Direction

- Toast bagel.
- Spread with creamed cheese.
- Put bacon and egg between two halves of the bagel
- Share with a friend.

Index

A
Almond 3,9
Apple 3,7

B
Bacon 3,4
Bagel 3,9,24
Banana 3,4,16,20
Beer 3,18
Blueberry 3,5
Bran 3,11,23
Bread 1,3,4,7,8,9,11,15,16,18,19,20,23
Buns 3,10,13
Butter 3,5,9,17

C
Caramel 3,10
Carrot 3,8
Cheddar 3,6,12,23
Cheese 3,6,12
Chocolate 3,6,11
Cinnamon 3,4,5,7,8,10,14,17,21
Coconut 3,9
Cream 6,11

E
Egg 7

F
Flour 5

J
Jam 3,7,11
Jus 9

L
Lemon 3,11,13,24

M
Marmalade 17
Muffins 3,7,10,16

O
Oatmeal 3,14,15
Oil 18
Onion 3,6
Orange 3,16,22

P
Peach 3,17
Peanut butter 11
Port 3,17
Potato 3,8
Praline 3,16
Pumpkin 3,8,18

S
Sausage 24
Strawberry 3,22
Sugar 3,5,10,11

T
Tea 9,24
Tomato 24

V
Vegan 3,23

W
Walnut 3,18,23

Conclusion

Thank you again for downloading this book!

I hope you enjoyed reading about my book!

If you enjoyed this book, please take the time to share your thoughts and post a review on Amazon. It'd be greatly appreciated!

Write me an honest review about the book – I truly value your opinion and thoughts and I will incorporate them into my next book, which is already underway.

Thank you!

If you have any questions, **feel free to contact at:** *author@rosemaryrecipes.com*

Lula Chambers

rosemaryrecipes.com

Made in the USA
Las Vegas, NV
13 October 2024

96679415R00017